SCHOLASTIC News Nonfiction Readers®

W9-BRP-459

What's in Washington, D.C.?

By Laine Falk

Children's Press®
An Imprint of Scholastic Inc.
New York Toronto London Auckland Sydney
Mexico City New Delhi Hong Kong
Danbury, Connecticut

These content vocabulary word builders are for grades 1–2.

Subject Consultant: Eli J. Lesser, MA, Director of Education, National Constitution Center, Philadelphia, Pennsylvania

Reading Consultant: Cecilia Minden-Cupp, PhD, Early Literacy Consultant and Author, Chapel Hill, North Carolina

Photographs © 2009: Alamy Images: 5 top left, 8 (Yvonne Duffe), 23 bottom left (David R. Frazier Photolibrary, Inc.), back cover, 2, 4 top, 14 (Andre Jenny), 5 bottom right, 6 (Pictures Colour Library), 9 (Frank Vetere); AP Images/Lawrence Jackson: 23 bottom right; Corbis Images: 4 bottom right, 16 (Jessie Cohen/epa), 5 bottom left, 18 (Najlah Feanny); Danita Delimont Stock Photography: 5 top right, 10 (Dennis Flaherty/ Bill Jaynes Gallery), 15 (David R. Frazier); Getty Images: 11 (Uyen Le), cover (Vincent Ricardel), 23 top left (Alex Wong); Masterfile: 1, 7; Photoshot: 19 (Bloomberg News/Landov), 23 top right (World Pictures); Smithsonian Institution, Washington, DC/National Air and Space Museum: 13 (Mark Avino), 4 bottom left, 12 (Eric Long); Smithsonian's National Zoo/Ann Batdorf: 17; The Granger Collection, New York/ Gilbert Stuart: 11 inset; Maps by James McMahon (additional art pages 20-21 by Lucas Aoki)

Series Design: Simonsays Design!
Art Direction, Production, and Digital Imaging: Scholastic Classroom Magazines

Library of Congress Cataloging-in-Publication Data

Falk, Laine, 1974-
What's in Washington, D.C.? / Laine Falk.
    p. cm. – (Scholastic news nonfiction readers)
Includes bibliographical references and index.
ISBN 13: 978-0-531-21092-5 (lib. bdg.)   978-0-531-22429-8 (pbk.)
ISBN 10: 0-531-21092-8 (lib. bdg.)   0-531-22429-5 (pbk.)
    1. Washington (D.C.)–Description and travel–Juvenile literature. I. Title. II. Series.
F194.3.F35 2009
917.5304'42–dc22   2008027083

1 2 3 4 5 6 7 8 9 10 R 18 17 16 15 14 13 12 11 10 09

CONTENTS

WORD HUNT

Look for these words as you read. They will be in **bold**.

blossoms
(**bloss**-uhmz)

museum
(myoo-**zee**-uhm)

pandas
(**pan**-duhz)

4

Capitol
(**kap**-uh-tuhl)

monument
(**mon**-yuh-muhnt)

subway
(**suhb**-way)

White House
(wite houss)

What's in Washington, D.C.?

The home of our President is in Washington, D.C. It is called the **White House**.

What else can you find in Washington, D.C.?

White House

The White House is in Washington, D.C., the nation's capital.

United States

Atlantic Ocean

★ Washington, D.C.

North
West ◆ East

You can find the U.S. **Capitol**. Many of our leaders work there. They help make our laws.

The round part on top of the Capitol is called a dome.

Capitol

Leaders from all 50 states work in the Capitol. The laws they help make are rules for everyone to follow.

Look at the tallest building in the city! It is the Washington **Monument**.

There are 50 flags around it. They stand for the 50 states in the United States.

monument

George Washington

The Washington Monument is 555 feet tall! It was built to honor George Washington, our first President.

You can visit a **museum**. There are many museums in Washington, D.C. At this one, you can see airplanes and rocket ships!

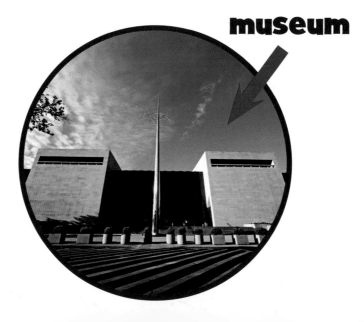

museum

People come from all over to visit the National Air and Space Museum.

Long ago, the people of Japan [juh-PAN] gave the city a gift. They gave cherry trees! The trees bloom in spring. People enjoy their pink and white **blossoms**.

blossoms

These kids smell the cherry blossoms. How do you think the flowers smell?

Japan

U.S.

Pacific Ocean

You can find **pandas** in the city, too. They live in the zoo. It is one of the few zoos in the country where pandas live.

pandas

Munch, munch! Pandas love to eat bamboo. People love to watch.

You can't find this last thing *in* Washington, D.C. It is *under* it!

The **subway** is a train. It runs under the city. You can take the subway to see all the things that are in Washington, D.C.!

subway

The people in Washington, D.C., call their subway the Metro.

WHAT CAN YOU FIND

How many buildings can you name on the m[o]

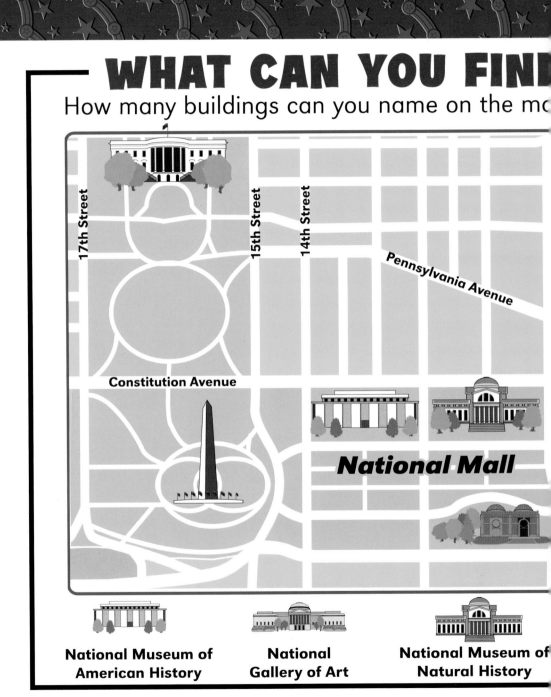

17th Street

15th Street

14th Street

Pennsylvania Avenue

Constitution Avenue

National Mall

**National Museum of
American History**

**National
Gallery of Art**

**National Museum of
Natural History**

se the pictures to help you.

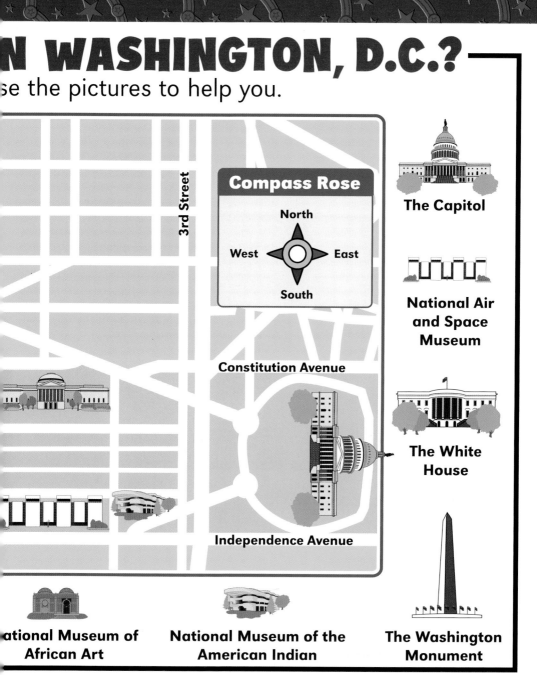

Compass Rose

North

West • East

South

3rd Street

Constitution Avenue

Independence Avenue

The Capitol

National Air and Space Museum

The White House

ational Museum of African Art

National Museum of the American Indian

The Washington Monument

YOUR NEW WORDS

blossoms (**bloss**-uhmz) flowers on a fruit tree

Capitol (**kap**-uh-tuhl) the building where part of the U.S. government meets and works

monument (**mon**-yuh-muhnt) a statue or a building that is meant to remind us of a person or of something that happened

museum (myoo-**zee**-uhm) a place to see things from art, history, or science

pandas (**pan**-duhz) animals that look like bears and have thick black and white fur

subway (**suhb**-way) trains that run underground in a city

White House (wite houss) the home and office of the United States President

WHAT ELSE IS IN WASHINGTON, D.C.?

The Bureau of Engraving and Printing

The Lincoln Memorial

Museum of the American Indian

The Potomac River

INDEX

FIND OUT MORE

Book:
Curlee, Lynn. *Capital*. New York: Atheneum, 2003.

Website:
Washington, D.C., for Kids!
http://kids.dc.gov

MEET THE AUTHOR
Laine Falk was born in Washington, D.C., and grew up nearby in Maryland. She lives in New York with her family.